A CENTURY *of* BATH

A pre-First World War view looking up Union Street from Stall Street. (*Bath Reference Library*)

A CENTURY *of* BATH

DAVID & JONATHAN FALCONER

SUTTON PUBLISHING

First published in the United Kingdom in 1999 by
Sutton Publishing Limited · Phoenix Mill
Thrupp · Stroud · Gloucestershire · GL5 2BU

British Library Cataloguing in Publication Data
A catalogue record for this book is available from the British Library.

ISBN 0-7509-2442-X

Front endpaper: Bath from the south-east, August 1920. Among the city's landmarks can be seen the Empire Hotel (top right) above the river, its proportions detracting from the commanding presence of the Abbey at the centre of the picture. The cloister vestry on the south side of the Abbey's nave, a memorial to the dead of the First World War, had yet to be built (1923). To the east of the Abbey is the Royal Literary and Scientific Institution (demolished 1932–3), and below it Institution Gardens (now Parade Gardens). At the bottom left is St James's Church (now demolished), and to its right Weymouth House School. The attractive gardens at the bottom right are now occupied by an incongruous late-twentieth century car park. (*Aerofilms Ltd*)
Back endpaper: Central Bath seen from a hot air balloon in September 1998. In the foreground can be seen the Rec, Johnstone Street and Laura Place, with Argyle Street leading to Pulteney Bridge. On the city side of the river from left to right are Parade Gardens, Pierrepont Street, Orange Grove, the Abbey, the newly converted Empire, the Guildhall, Market, and Victoria Art Gallery, High Street and Bridge Street, and the back of the Podium. (*Janet Rayner*)
Half title page: An electric tram passes along the High Street in the mid-1930s, framed by the entrance to the Guildhall Market. (*Bath Reference Library*)
Title page: A timeless vista of the northern slopes of the city looking towards St Stephen's Church and the Royal School, August 1999. (*Annie Falconer*)

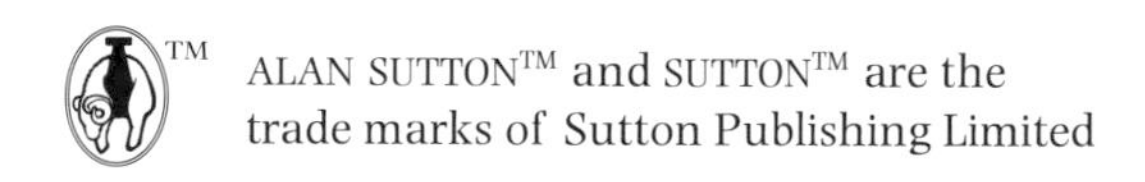

ALAN SUTTON™ and SUTTON™ are the trade marks of Sutton Publishing Limited

George V visits the Roman Baths, 9 November 1917. (*Bath City Archives*)

Typeset in 11/14pt Photina.
Typesetting and origination by
Sutton Publishing Limited.
Printed in Great Britain by
The Bath Press, Bath.

Contents

Westgate Street, 1925. Sydney Bush's grocery store on the right of the photograph gave the corner its name of 'Bush's Corner'. Today the premises are occupied by Pizza Hut. On the corner of Westgate Street and Westgate Buildings can be seen Barnes' tobacconist shop, now occupied by the Bottoms Up off-licence. (*Bath Reference Library*)

Britain: A Century of Change

Children gathered around an early wireless set in the 1920s. The speed and forms of communication were to change dramatically as the century advanced. (*Barnaby's Picture Library*)

The delirious rejoicing at the news of the Relief of Mafeking, during the Boer War in May 1900, is a colourful historical moment. But, in retrospect, the introduction that year of the first motor bus was rather more important, signalling another major adjustment to town life. In the previous 60 years railway stations, post-and-telegraph offices, police and fire stations, gas works and gasometers, new livestock markets and covered markets, schools, churches, football grounds, hospitals and asylums, water pumping stations and sewerage plants had totally altered the urban scene, as the country's population tripled and over 70 per cent were born in or moved to the towns.

When Queen Victoria died in 1901, she was measured for her coffin by her grandson Kaiser Wilhelm, the London prostitutes put on black mourning and the blinds came down in the villas and terraces spreading out from the old town centres. These centres were reachable by train and tram, by the new bicycles and still newer motor cars, connected by the new telephone, and lit by gas or even electricity. The shops may have been full of British-made cotton and woollen clothing but the grocers and butchers were selling cheap Danish bacon, Argentinian beef, Australasian mutton, tinned or dried fish and fruit from Canada, California and South Africa. Most of these goods were carried in British-built-and-crewed ships, burning Welsh steam coal.

Women working as porters on the Great Western Railway, Paddington, *c.* 1917. (*W.L. Kenning/ Adrian Vaughan Collection*)

As the first decade moved on, the Open Spaces Act meant more parks, bowling greens and cricket pitches. The first state pensions came in, together with higher taxation and death duties. These were raised mostly to pay for the new Dreadnought battleships needed to maintain naval superiority over Germany, and deter them from war. But the deterrent did not work. The First World War transformed the place of women, as they took over many men's jobs. Its other legacies were the war memorials which joined the statues of Victorian worthies in main squares round the land. After 1918 death duties bit even harder and a quarter of England changed hands in a few years.

The multiple shop – the chain store – appeared in the high street: Sainsburys, Maypole, Lipton's, Home & Colonial, the Fifty Shilling Tailor, Burton, Boots, W.H. Smith. The shopper was spoilt for choice, attracted by the brash fascias and advertising hoardings for national brands like Bovril, Pears Soap, and Ovaltine. Many new buildings began to be seen, such as garages, motor showrooms, picture palaces (cinemas), 'palais de dance', and the bow-windowed, pebble-dashed, tile-hung, half-timbered houses that were built as ribbon-development along the roads and new bypasses or on the new estates nudging the green belts.

During the 1920s cars became more reliable and sophisticated as well as commonplace, with developments like the electric self-starter making them easier for women to drive. Who wanted to turn a crank handle in the new short skirt? This was, indeed, the electric age as much as the motor era. Trolley buses, electric trams and trains extended mass transport and electric light replaced gas in the street and the home, which itself was groomed by the vacuum cleaner.

Father and child cycling past Buckingham Palace on VE Day, 8 May 1945. (*Hulton Getty Picture Collection*)

A major jolt to the march onward and upward was administered by the Great Depression of the early 1930s. The older British industries – textiles, shipbuilding, iron, steel, coal – were already under pressure from foreign competition when this worldwide slump arrived, cutting exports by half in two years and producing 3 million unemployed (and still rising) by 1932. Luckily there were new diversions to alleviate the misery. The 'talkies' arrived in the cinemas; more and more radios and gramophones were to be found in people's homes; there were new women's magazines, with fashion, cookery tips and problem pages; football pools; the flying feats of women pilots like Amy Johnson; the Loch Ness Monster; cheap chocolate and the drama of Edward VIII's abdication.

Things were looking up again by 1936 and unemployment was down to 2 million. New light industry was booming in the Home Counties as factories struggled to keep up with the demand for radios, radiograms, cars and electronic goods including the first television sets. The threat from Hitler's Germany meant rearmament, particularly of the airforce, which stimulated aircraft and aero engine firms. If you were lucky and lived in the south, there was good money to be earned. A semi-detached house cost £450, a Morris Cowley £150. People may have smoked like chimneys but life expectancy, since 1918, was up by 15 years while the birth rate had almost halved. The fifty-four hour week was down to forty-eight hours and there were 9 million radio licences by 1939.

In some ways it is the little memories that seem to linger longest from the Second World War: the kerbs painted white to show up in the blackout, the rattle of ack-ack shrapnel on roof tiles, sparrows killed by bomb blast, painting your legs brown and then adding a black seam

A family gathered around their television set in the 1950s. (*Hulton Getty Picture Collection*)

down the back to simulate stockings. The biggest damage, apart from London, was in the south-west (Plymouth, Bristol) and the Midlands (Coventry, Birmingham). Postwar reconstruction was rooted in the Beveridge Report which set out the expectations for the Welfare State. This, together with the nationalisation of the Bank of England, coal, gas, electricity and the railways, formed the programme of the Labour government in 1945. At this time the USA was calling in its debts and Britain was beggared by the war, yet still administering its Empire.

Times were hard in the late 1940s, with rationing even more stringent than during the war. Yet this was, as has been said, 'an innocent and well-behaved era'. The first let-up came in 1951 with the Festival of Britain and then there was another fillip in 1953 from the Coronation, which incidentally gave a huge boost to the spread of TV. By 1954 leisure motoring had been resumed but the Comet – Britain's best hope for taking on the American aviation industry – suffered a series of mysterious crashes. The Suez debacle of 1956 was followed by an acceleration in the withdrawal from Empire, which had begun in 1947 with the Independence of India. Consumerism was truly born with the advent of commercial TV and most homes soon boasted washing machines, fridges, electric irons and fires.

The *Lady Chatterley* obscenity trial in 1960 was something of a straw in the wind for what was to follow in that decade. A collective loss of inhibition seemed to sweep the land, as stately home owners opened up, the Beatles and the Rolling Stones transformed popular music, and retailing, cinema and the theatre were revolutionised. Designers, hairdressers, photographers and models moved into places vacated by an Establishment put to flight by the new breed of satirists spawned by *Beyond the Fringe* and *Private Eye*.

In the 1970s Britain seems to have suffered a prolonged hangover after the excesses of the previous decade. Ulster, inflation and union troubles were not made up for by entry into the EEC, North Sea Oil, Women's Lib or, indeed, Punk Rock. Mrs Thatcher applied the corrective in the 1980s, as the country moved more and more from its old manufacturing base over to providing services, consulting, advertising, and expertise in the 'invisible' market of high finance or in IT. Britain entertained the world with *Cats*, *Phantom of the Opera*, *Four Weddings and a Funeral*, *The Full Monty*, *Mr Bean* and the *Teletubbies*.

The post-1945 townscape has seen changes to match those in the worlds of work, entertainment and politics. In 1956 the Clean Air Act served notice on smogs and pea-souper fogs, smuts and blackened buildings, forcing people to stop burning coal and go over to smokeless sources of heat and energy. In the same decade some of the best urban building took place in the 'new towns' like Basildon, Crawley, Stevenage and Harlow. Elsewhere open warfare was declared on slums and what was labelled inadequate, cramped, back-to-back, two-up, two-down, housing. The new 'machine for living in' was a flat in a high-rise block. The architects and planners who promoted these were in league with the traffic engineers, determined to keep the motor car moving whatever the price in multi-storey car parks, meters, traffic wardens and ring roads.

Carnaby Street in the 1960s. (*Barnaby's Picture Library*)

The Millennium Dome at Greenwich, 1999. (*Michael Durnan/Barnaby's Picture Library*)

The old pollutant, coal smoke, was replaced by petrol and diesel exhaust, and traffic noise. Even in the back garden it was hard to find peace as motor mowers, then leaf blowers and strimmers made themselves heard, and the neighbours let you share their choice of music from their powerful new amplifiers, whether you wanted to or not. Fast food was no longer only a pork pie in a pub or fish-and-chips. There were Indian curry houses, Chinese take-aways and American-style hamburgers, while the drinker could get away from beer in a wine bar. Under the impact of television the big Gaumonts and Odeons closed or were rebuilt as multi-screen cinemas, while the palais de dance gave way to discos and clubs.

From the late 1960s the introduction of listed buildings and conservation areas, together with the growth of preservation societies, put a brake on 'comprehensive redevelopment'. Now the new risk at the end of the 1990s is that town centres may die, as shoppers are attracted to the edge-of-town supermarkets surrounded by parking space, where much more than food and groceries can be bought. The ease of the one-stop shop represents the latest challenge to the good health of our towns. But with care, ingenuity and a determination to keep control of our environment, this challenge can be met.

Bath: An Introduction

With the death of Her Imperial Majesty Queen Victoria in the first year of the twentieth century, an era drew to a close. The nineteenth century had seen the expansion and the glory days of the greatest empire in the history of the world – the British Empire – on which, it was said, the sun never set. (The city of Bath raised a formidable looking hotel in its name in 1901 – the Empire Hotel.) The closing years of that century saw the outbreak of the largest and most costly war in which the British had been engaged since the time of Napoleon. The South African, or Boer, War saw the deployment of half a million men against a force of little more than 88,000 Boers. Bath men served as combatants in a number of local regiments, and as doctors and medical attendants with the Royal Army Medical Corps and the St John Ambulance Brigade. In 1903, General Lord Methuen, who had taken part in the campaign, unveiled a war memorial in the Guildhall to commemorate the Volunteers who had left the city in 1900 for active service in South Africa.

With the death of Victoria in 1901 came a new king, the popular and affable Edward VII, who had waited long years in the wings. His reign proved to be a brief yet lively one. At Edward's death in 1910, George V ascended the throne and it was during his reign that Britain again became embroiled in a terrible conflict, this time on an epic scale. In August 1914 the First World War broke out, and for over four years its brutality touched the lives of nearly every man, woman and child in the land. A glance at the Bath War Memorial at the Queens Parade entrance to the Royal Victoria Park gives an idea of the sacrifice made by Bath families – it lists the names of 1,200 Bath men who were killed. At the time, it was described as 'the war to end all wars'. But, alas, that was not to be so.

The eighteenth- and nineteenth-century ethos of Bath as an English spa *par excellence* was, to some extent, dissipated by the social changes that resulted from the First World War. Fierce competition from the continental spas of Baden-Baden and Aix-les-Bains pulled the first of several plugs in Bath's leaking spa economy. A brief recovery was made between the wars, but the revival, such as it was, proved short-lived.

A growth in industry and commerce ensured that Bath did not fade into obscurity, despite its impending decline as a spa resort. Sir Isaac Pitman established his printing and publishing business in the Lower Bristol Road at East Twerton, and the heavy engineering firm of Stothert & Pitt (also on the Lower Bristol Road) achieved an enviable reputation as crane builders to the world. At their Newbridge works, the Horstmann Gear Co. manufactured precision instruments and mechanisms, while across the river at Twerton the cloth trade, for which Bath had been well known in the sixteenth century, continued to flourish at Carr's Mill. Nearby, skilled craftsmen at Bath Cabinet Makers continued their trade

The grand finale of the Bath Pageant in Victoria Park, 1909. In a series of tableaux, the history of the city was re-enacted from Roman times to the Regency period. (*Bath Reference Library*)

of coach building and cabinet making. Alongside the canal at Bathampton, Harbutt's produced Plasticine, their famous modelling material. During the Second World War, all of these Bath companies were to play a full and vital role in the nation's war effort.

The rise of Nazism in Germany during the 1930s led to the outbreak of a second devastating world war in September 1939. Although London had suffered air raids during the First World War, this time many of the major cities in the country were to be visited by German bombers, dealing terrible loss of life to the civilian population, and widespread destruction of property. Although it was not an obvious target, the undefended city of Bath suffered two nights of murderous bombing in April 1942. This was the so-called 'Baedeker' blitz mounted in retaliation for the RAF's raids on the historic German towns of Rostock and Lübeck. The Book of Remembrance in Bath Abbey bears silent testimony to the tragic loss of more than 400 lives in the city.

Miraculously, at the heart of Bath, the Abbey, Roman Baths, Pump Room and Guildhall were not hit in the bombing, but the recently restored Assembly Rooms and several historic houses, including the Elizabethan Hetling House (Abbey Church House), were severely damaged and had to be rebuilt. Residential property in the Julian Road,

A chequered flag marks the site of an unexploded bomb at Lansdown Place East following the 'Baedeker' blitz on Bath, 25 27 April 1942. (*Bath Reference Library*)

Kingsmead and Green Park areas suffered greatly from the effects of high explosive and incendiary bombs, while Bath's western suburbs also received extensive bomb damage. Three city churches, St Andrew's, St James's, and Holy Trinity, and one chapel, All Saints', of which only the shells remained, were later demolished.

After the destruction of or damage to many thousands of buildings in the blitz, a comprehensive planning review of the city was called for, and Sir Patrick Abercrombie conceived a blueprint for its future 'development'. Published in 1945, it was called *A Plan for Bath*, and although given serious consideration it was never implemented. Following the euphoria of victory over the Axis powers in the summer of 1945, the city of Bath, in common with the rest of the country, settled down in sober mood to contemplate the future.

The huge influx of Admiralty personnel and essential workers to Bath at the outbreak of war had seen most of the city's major hotels requisitioned 'for the duration'; but for many years after peace was restored they were retained by the Admiralty as office accommodation. The fragile recovery enjoyed by the spa city between the wars went into sharp decline in the late 1940s and '50s, due largely to the shortage of good hotels upon which it depended to accommodate its visitors.

The slanting rays of the evening sun light up this unusual view of the Circus, photographed from a hot air balloon in September 1998. (*Janet Rayner*)

In an attempt to bolster the city's economy, Bath turned to the emerging tourist trade – short-stay 'package tour' visitors of all kinds and from all parts of the world. It is evident that the new type of visitor has been the salvation of the city in economic terms, but in some ways this sort of tourism has had a deleterious effect on the character of Bath. It is now plain to see that there are few shops in the city centre that cater for the daily needs of Bathonians. Many shopkeepers have turned to the lucrative tourist trade with its insatiable demand for souvenirs and knick-knacks. The tour buses that grind their way around the city also do a roaring trade, but attract complaints from residents about exhaust pollution, and the volume of the amplified voices of their tour guides. It seems, though, that these things are here to stay for the foreseeable future.

For many years, thanks to the high-speed rail link with London, Bath has been a desirable place for commuters to live. But since the opening of the M4 motorway in the 1960s, linking London with the West Country, Bath's popularity as a commuter city and weekend playground for Londoners has steadily grown. But this popularity has proved a mixed blessing: the city and its environs have seen the cost of residential properties soar, and Bath now has some of the highest property prices outside London.

Ever since the arrival of speculators in the eighteenth century, successive generations have sought to put their stamp on the architectural face of the city. During the great building programmes of the eighteenth century, much of medieval Bath was swept away and replaced with the precise classical forms for which the city is internationally renowned today. The Victorians cleaned up much of 'old' Bath, and in its place erected their pseudo-Gothic and Italianate visions, and monstrosities such as the Empire Hotel. Each period has contributed in its own way, for better or for worse, to the buildings of the city.

But the greatest – and officially sanctioned – desecration of Bath's architectural heritage, begun early in the twentieth century, reached the apogee of its almost unbelievable civic philistinism during the 1960s. Literally thousands of buildings of architectural merit were unceremoniously torn down and replaced by what can charitably be described as vile excrescences on the face of what had once been a beautiful city – even with its warts!

Had it not been for the sometimes lone voices of the Bath Preservation Trust and a handful of conservationists – no doubt despised by those with avaricious eyes – it is not inconceivable that some of the jewels in Bath's architectural crown (those that we take for granted today) would have been 'carted away on developer's lorry' and replaced by clones of the Snow Hill flats or the Walcot Street Hilton Hotel. Even so, for many years to come Bathonians will have to live with the planning inanities in the Julian Road and Ballance Street area, Rosewell Court and the telephone exchange and Social Security offices, and other so-called 'developments' in the Monmouth Street, Charles Street and James Street West area.

The ease and convenience of travel has been greatly extended by the fast-growing ownership of cars, with the result that people no longer need to live where they work. As the century draws to its close, it is plain that our blind obsession with the internal combustion engine has allowed us to become subjugated to its tyranny. The motor car has become the great status symbol of our time. The old streets of central Bath were not designed for the type or volume of traffic we experience today; street congestion and air pollution are the orders of the day. Witness the almost endless daily congestion of traffic in Sydney Place, Bathwick Street and Cleveland Bridge heading for the M4 motorway.

Irreversible damage is being done not only to public health, but also to the fabric of buildings with levels of air pollutants often in excess of what is considered safe. Walking in and crossing the streets of Bath is fraught with danger, especially for young children and the elderly. But, thankfully, common sense is about to prevail! The city authorities are at last seriously considering restricting the movement of cars and motorcycles (but not buses) in certain city centre streets. Naturally, in the face of an imagined threat to their livelihoods, there has been an outcry from city traders who fear that such restrictions on the movement of cars will stop people shopping in Bath. But, if people want to continue to shop in Bath, they will do so – a fact proved in other historic towns and cities that have adopted similar schemes. It is the long-term interest of Bath that must be addressed. If Bath is not to be suffocated to death by its love affair with the car, then a drastic remedy is needed – and fast.

The long tradition of healing, begun in the first millennium, continues at the Royal National Hospital for Rheumatic Diseases, founded in the eighteenth century as the

Mineral Water Hospital, and at the more recently established Royal United Hospital situated on the city outskirts at Combe Park.

The late twentieth century has seen Bath emerge as a centre of higher and further education, with two universities and a college of further education. Although a designated World Heritage city that hosts a prestigious international arts festival every year, the city has no purpose-built concert hall. It can, however, lay claim to a world class rugby football team.

In recent years Bath has managed to reinvent itself as a fashionable place in which to live. Commerce continues to thrive and tourism is booming. A multi-million pound scheme to revive the city's spa has begun; and plans are well advanced to replace the hideous Southgate Street shopping centre with what – one hopes – will be a development more in keeping with the city's architectural heritage, and responsive to the needs of its residents.

For the past 500 years the noble Abbey church, dedicated to St Peter and St Paul, has stood as a commanding presence at the heart of the city. A haven from the frantic and materialistic world, it serves to remind us that the approaching millennium is a Christian celebration. Commercial hype has already tended to overshadow this fact, and it will probably be forgotten by the majority of people during the celebrations in Bath as elsewhere in the world. But the new century and millennium offer us all an opportunity for a new beginning.

End of an Era

The Bath Historical Pageant of 1909 re-enacted the history of the city from Roman times to the Regency period. (*Bath Reference Library*)

The classic picture-postcard panorama of the city of Bath from Beechen Cliff, seen here at the turn of the nineteenth century. One hundred years later, Beechen Cliff remains a popular vantage-point from which to photograph the city. (*Authors*)

News of the Relief of Mafeking by Kitchener and Roberts during the South African War was received by telegram at the Bath offices of the *Daily Chronicle and Argus* just before 10 pm on Friday 18 May 1900. In this picture a newsboy sells the 'war edition'. Bath sent hundreds of men to fight in the Boer War. (*Gwatkin/Bath and County Graphic*)

An early twentieth-century view of the west front of the Abbey across Abbey Church Yard, taken from the Grand Pump Room Hotel (demolished in 1958–9). On the right, beyond the colonnade (1786) can be seen the Pump Room (1791), and the late nineteenth-century Pump Room Annexe. (*W. Williams/R. and S. Withey*)

Laura Place and Great Pulteney Street pictured here towards the end of Victoria's reign at the turn of the nineteenth century. At the left of the picture is the entrance to the Pulteney Hotel. The Victorian fountain in the centre was demolished in the 1970s – in windy weather water was blown on to the windscreens of passing cars – and replaced by a lower fountain. To the right of the picture is the carriage office with a waiting hackney cab, and a bath chair. (*W. Williams/R. and S. Withey*)

This beautifully liveried Bath Road Car & Tram Co. horse tram was photographed at the Grosvenor terminus around the turn of the century. The first regular service of electric trams in the city on 2 January 1904 spelt the end of the road for horse trams like this one. (*Bath Reference Library*)

This turn of the century photograph shows the fine sweep of Royal Crescent with the spire of St Andrew's Church rising behind the roof-tops. (*W. Williams/Authors*)

The River Avon and Institution Gardens (now called Parade Gardens) as seen in the late nineteenth century from North Parade bridge. In front of the Abbey stands the Bath Royal Literary and Scientific Institution. (*W. Williams/R. and S. Withey*)

The Park Dairy (belonging to Park Farm) in Victoria Park, opposite the obelisk commemorating the accession of Queen Victoria, 1902. At that time, and within living memory, cows were grazed on the Middle Common and brought down Cow Lane (which links the Common with the bottom of Marlborough Buildings) for milking. (*W. Rossiter/Bath and County Graphic*)

Laying the foundation stone of the Weymouth House School on 5 April 1897. The school, situated behind St James's Street, was demolished in 1961. Under the foundation stone was found a time capsule containing a document, copies of *Keene's Bath Journal* for 2 and 9 May 1896, a portrait of the Marquess of Bath, two Victorian coins, and a diamond jubilee medal of Queen Victoria. The site was purchased to enable a big development scheme by Marks & Spencer and F.W. Woolworth in the area bounded by Abbey Gate Street, New Orchard Street, and Stall Street. (*Bath Reference Library*)

Pupils at their desks in Weymouth House School fix their gaze on an Edwardian photographer who has given them a few moments respite from the 'three Rs'. None could have foreseen that 40 years later their school would be used as a temporary mortuary for Bath's blitz dead. (*Bath Reference Library*)

In this tantalising glimpse of a lost corner of Bath, pupils huddle in the playground near the gateway of Weymouth House School in Abbey Gate Street. The building to the right beyond the gate is now occupied by Evans' Fish and Chip Restaurant. In the background is Abbey Green, with its still familiar plane tree, planted in 1880 by Mr Jefferys, a sweep who lived at 2A Abbey Green, at its centre. (*Bath Reference Library*)

Weymouth House from St James's Street in 1941. This was the town house of the Thynne family of Longleat. Viscount Weymouth, who was born in 1734, and died in 1796 seven years after being created Marquis of Bath, occasionally lived here. (*Bath Reference Library*)

Carriages and a motor car (far left) await the arrival of passengers at the Great Western Railway station (*c.* 1900). The line from Bristol to Bath was opened in 1840, and the following year the line from Bath to London. The Great Western Railway Company built Manvers Street and half of Dorchester Street to give access to the station. (*Colin Maggs*)

An early twentieth-century house party at Cranwells in Weston Road, the home of Mr S. Campbell Cory JP, DL. The house was formerly the home of Sir Jerom Murch, a Bath worthy and former mayor. (*Bath and County Graphic*)

Lines for electric trams being laid in London Street, Walcot, during 1903. The building with the long frontage at the right of the picture later became The Hat and Feather public house. In the background (left) on the high pavement is Walcot Parade. (*Colin Maggs*)

An electric tram at the bottom of Guinea Lane heading for Bathford. Beyond and above Hedgemead Park is Camden Crescent. (*Postcard/Authors*)

This fully laden double-decker bus (registration FB 07), standing on New Bridge on the western outskirts of Bath, prepares to take a party of well-dressed men on a special excursion in 1907. The photograph carries no further details, but some of the men wear buttonholes. (*Colin Maggs*)

Restoration work on the east end and tower of the Abbey in 1906 forms an imposing backdrop to the coach and coachman, the uniformed commissionaire from the Empire Hotel, and the fine 4½-litre 4-cylinder 1904 Renault motor car, registration number 844 E7. (*Bath Chronicle*)

'Guinea Pig Jack', a well-known Bath character for many years, is seen here with his guinea pigs in Manvers Street in the early 1900s. Born in Italy, his real name was Dominice Oconia. The postcard bearing this photograph is postmarked Bath, 17 November 1905, and addressed to J.P.E. Falconer (father and grandfather to the authors). The message reads: 'Very much better & we hope to see him again with his pigs.' It has been annotated by the recipient, 'Guinea Pig Jack had been seriously ill.' He died in 1907. (*Authors*)

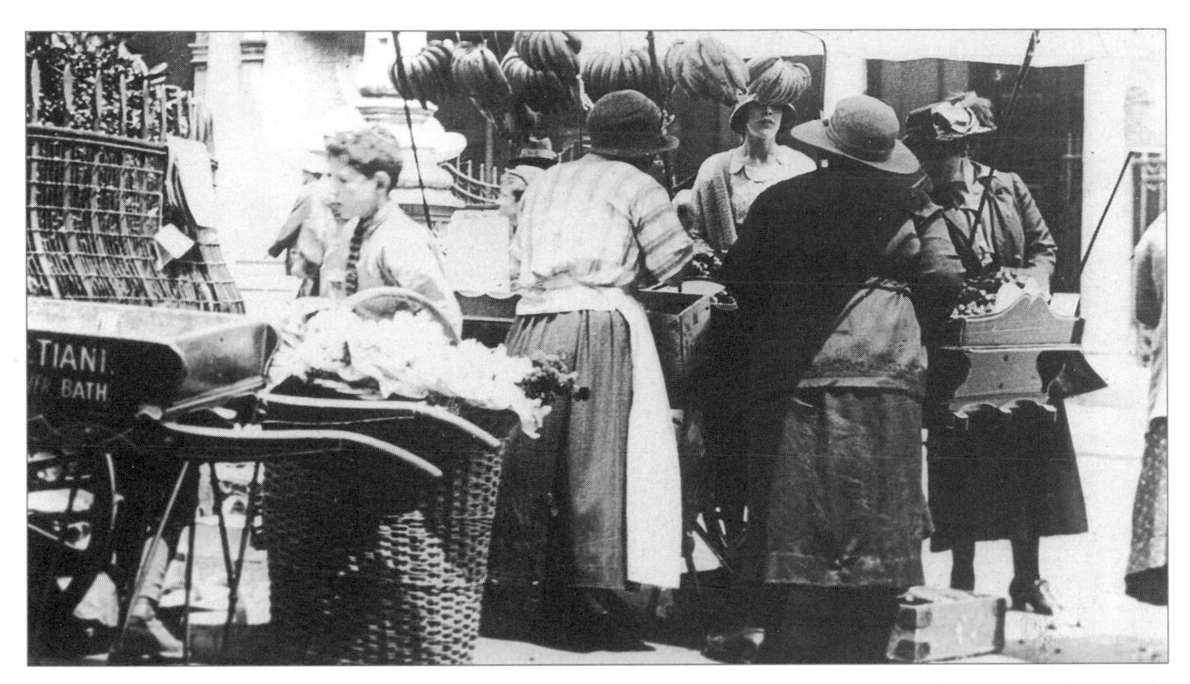

Bananas were plentiful at this street vendor's stall in Stall Street near the entrance to the King's and Queen's Baths in about 1912. To the left of the picture is the mineral water fountain (since removed to Parade Gardens) and a barrow belonging to A. Tiani, who later ran a milk and ice cream bar in Westgate Street. Stall Street took its name from the medieval church of St Mary de Stall which stood at the north-west corner of the present Abbey Church Yard. *(John Reynolds)*

This wonderfully evocative scene at the bottom of Southgate Street was taken in the early 1900s from the Old Bridge (demolished in the early 1960s). The church in the background is St James's, gutted by incendiary bombs during the Blitz of 1942 and later demolished. Behind the woman walking across the Old Bridge is the Full Moon Hotel on the corner of Dorchester Street. *(John Reynolds)*

The Sawclose early in the twentieth century. In the right background is the Blue Coat School (rebuilt in the mid-nineteenth century) formerly known as the Bath Charity School, it was founded in 1711 by Robert Nelson. To the left of the picture is Broadley's – a public house which still exists – and Drew Son & Butcher, corset manufacturers. (*Authors*)

Major C.E. Davis FSA (City Architect and architect of the Empire Hotel) made a considerable reputation for himself as the discoverer of the Roman Baths, and for his work in connection with the new Royal Baths; he died in 1902. (*Bath and County Graphic*)

The foundation stone of the Empire Hotel was laid in December 1899 on a site formerly occupied by old houses in Orange Grove Court. Two years later, 'amid the pealing of the Abbey bells, with flags and bunting fluttering', the 200-room Empire Hotel was opened and dedicated to the use of visitors to the city. A castle, mansion and cottage were incorporated in the design at roof level. The cost was £10,000. In this contemporary photograph taken from Spring Gardens Road can be seen Grand Parade, and the steeple of St Michael's Church. (*Bath and County Graphic*)

Jumping for the Coronation Prize of £50 at the 1902 Bath Horse Show at Lambridge. The show (now long since defunct) was held annually in the first week of September. Today, the former Horse Show Ground is used to train Bath's championship-winning rugby side. (*A.H. Hawke/Bath and County Graphic*)

The White Hart Hotel at the junction of Widcombe Hill and Prior Park Road in 1902. The original figure of a white hart (seen here over the doorway) was removed from the White Hart Inn of Dickens' fame (which occupied the site of its successor, the Grand Pump Room Hotel facing Abbey Church Yard) and purchased by Mr Hurd, proprietor of the White Hart, Widcombe. (*W.G. Lewis/Bath and County Graphic*)

Cricket enjoyed its heyday in England during the Edwardian era. Here are members of Bath Corporation Officers and Bath Police cricket teams who played each other in 1905. The fine selection of headwear is plain to see. (*Bath Reference Library*)

In 1903, the historic office of Master of Ceremonies, hitherto unoccupied for a number of years, was revived. (The most famous of Bath's MCs was Richard 'Beau' Nash who was appointed in 1704.) The new MC was Alderman Major Charles Simpson JP (seen in the front row wearing his badge of office). On 13 April 1903, a highly successful Fancy Dress Easter Monday Ball was held at the Assembly Rooms with Major Simpson presiding. This photograph of the Grand Assembly was taken on that occasion. Two evenings later there was a second Easter Ball, in the form of a Private Subscription Ball, 'distinguished by a novelty in the way of a Cake Walk, the intricacies of which . . . were quite unknown in Beau Nash's day'! (*Graystone Bird/Bath and County Graphic*)

The stage and interior of the Palace Vaudeville Theatre (1903). Formerly known as the Pavilion, and the Lyric Music Hall, it was reopened as the Palace Vaudeville Theatre in 1903. The Palace (as it was popularly known) offered two performances a night. Among other innovations was the provision of a new saloon bar in order to do away with the contemporary fashion of drinking in the auditorium. The Palace enjoyed great popularity for many years until dwindling audiences forced its closure. It was later reopened as a bingo hall. Older Bathonians will have nostalgic memories of the Palace. (*Bath and County Graphic*)

'Canadian & American Representatives. Lady de Blaquiere as Mother Bath (England)': a tableau from the Bath Historical Pageant of 1909. Held under the patronage of the Duke and Duchess of Connaught, the pageant re-enacted the history of the city from Roman times to the Regency period. (*Lewis Bros/Bath Reference Library*)

The First World War

Wounded soldiers convalesce at Bath War Hospital, Combe Park. (*Bath Reference Library*)

While the guns rumbled in France and Belgium and soldiers went 'over the top' on the Western Front, at home in England tea on the Pump Room Terrace above the Great Roman Bath continued as usual. The young army officer on the extreme left wears the uniform of the South Staffordshire Regiment. In common with virtually every city, town and village across the land, many Bath families lost loved ones in the First World War. (*Bath Reference Library*)

The smartly attired stationmaster of the Midland Station (Green Park) and his staff pose for the camera in 1914. Behind them can be seen a group of hansom cabs waiting for hire. The Midland was served by two railway companies – the London, Midland & Scottish (LMS), and the Somerset & Dorset ('Slow and Dirty') – which ran between the Midlands and the south coast. (*Colin Maggs*)

Male and female engine cleaners with Somerset & Dorset 4–4–0 No. 71 at Bath during the First World War. It was during the war that women assumed many of the jobs originally undertaken by men, leading to further emancipation in the workplace and the vote for certain women over 30 in 1918. It was not until 1928 that all women over 21 were entitled to vote. (*Colin Maggs*)

The stern figure of the Matron of Bath War Hospital at Combe Park, pictured here with visitors. This temporary war hospital, opened in April 1916, was equipped with 1,000 beds and an operating theatre for wounded soldiers brought to Bath from the Western Front for treatment and to convalesce. (*Bath Reference Library*)

King George V and Queen Mary visited Bath on 9 November 1917 to inspect the Roman Baths and Pump Room. Here they are seen accompanied by the Mayor, Alderman C.H. Long. Across the Channel in France the war continued to rage on the Western Front. The Third Battle of Ypres – better known as Passchendaele – had drawn to a close on 6 November, with British and Empire casualties of half a million. On 20 November, the first great tank battle in history opened at Cambrai. (*Bath City Archives*)

Bath War
Hospital.
No. 3 Ward.

Most of the wounded soldiers who came to Bath were treated at the Bath War Hospital. Here is a group of soldiers and nurses in the hospital's No. 3 ward. (*Bath Reference Library*)

The killing is finally over: a seething mass of humanity gives thanks for the end of the First World War at an open-air service in front of Royal Crescent in 1919. More than 6 million soldiers were killed and another 14 million wounded in the so-called 'war to end all wars'. Bath alone lost close on 1,200 men. (*Bath Reference Library*)

BATH ELECTION, 1918.

THE COALITION CANDIDATE.

CAPT. C. T. FOXCROFT.

Printed and Published by F. C. Barber, at the "Bath and Wilts Chronicle" Office, 33, Westgate Street Bath.

'Vote for the Coalition candidate because the Coalition Government places the Empire before Party.' An election address delivered to Bath homes in November 1918, following the end of the First World War, canvassing votes in favour of Captain Charles Foxcroft, a supporter of the Coalition government 'under whose administration Victory has been achieved'. In later elections, Captain Foxcroft, who lived at 36 Brock Street, stood as a Conservative candidate. (*Authors*)

Indian Summer

Flags and bunting decorate Milsom Street to mark the Silver Jubilee of George V in 1935. (*Bath City Archives*)

Floods in the Dolemeads in 1925. The Dolemeads (now rebuilt), on the south-east bank of the River Avon, housed some of Bath's poorest families. Year after year they suffered the flooding of their dwellings. With the introduction of a flood prevention scheme during 1964–5, the annual flooding of areas close to the river, thankfully, became a thing of the past. (*Authors*)

Some of the mean tenements and their poor inhabitants in Milk Street (now demolished) in the 1930s. At the top end of the street at no. 10 was The Rose and Crown public house which closed in about 1939. Milk Street and Avon Street, which ran parallel with it, were among the poorest areas of Bath. (*Bath Reference Library*)

Taxis await the arrival of passengers at the Midland station, Green Park, 1922. (*Colin Maggs*)

Photographs of Kingsmead Street – seen here in 1922 – are very rare. The street was severely damaged during the 1942 blitz and no longer exists, due largely to the insensitivity of postwar planners who built a block of flats (Rosewell Court) and a car park at right angles across the route of the old street. (*Bath Reference Library*)

The Seven Dials public house (demolished in the 1930s) stood at the junction of Westgate Buildings, Westgate Street, Monmouth Street, and Kingsmead Square. At the top of the street (right) is the Theatre Royal, and next to it the Garrick's Head (formerly the residence of Beau Nash). Opposite the Garrick's Head was a public house called The Peep O'Day which finally called time to its customers in 1909–10. (*Bath Reference Library*)

A busy street scene in 1925 at the top of Southgate Street. A pair of trams, one entering the city from Weston village, the other heading for Twerton, rattle their way past the west door of St James's Church. On the extreme right of the picture can be seen Holloway's, the butchers. (*Bath Reference Library*)

The fine parish church of St James, Southgate, viewed from the Lower Borough Walls. The Gothic tower was rebuilt in 1716, and the body of the church in 1768–9. On the night of 26 April 1942 the church was set alight by incendiary bombs and the gutted ruin was finally demolished in 1959–60. On the site of the church new premises were erected for F.W. Woolworth Ltd. A recently extended Marks & Spencer store now occupies the site. To the right of the church is New Orchard Street South leading to Henry Street. In the distance can be seen the houses on the corner of Henry Street and Philip Street. (*Bath Reference Library*)

Union Street viewed from Stall Street in the early 1930s. To the right is the Pump Room Colonnade (1786). The sign on the wall at the left of the picture directs people to the Little Theatre News Cinema in St Michael's Place (still open in 1999). Beyond is the entrance to the New Royal Baths, next to the Grand Pump Room Hotel (not visible). On the left-hand side of Union Street is Lipton's grocery shop, and beyond it James Colmer's department store. The electric tram in the foreground is heading for Combe Down. (*Bath Reference Library*)

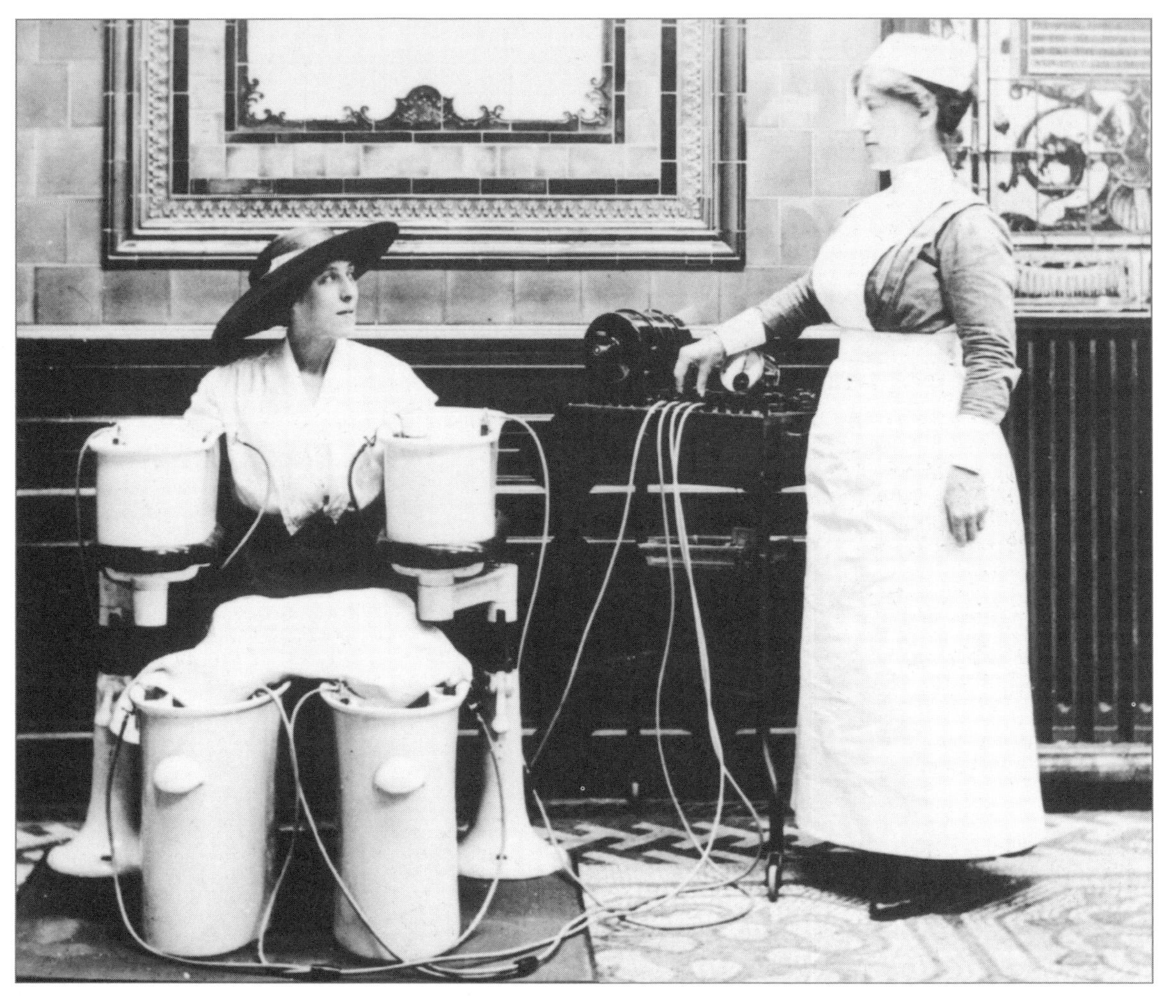

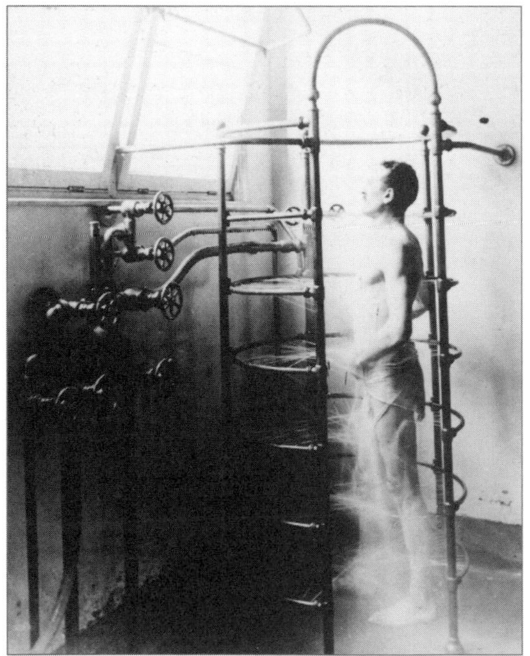

Above: Bath's longstanding reputation as a spa resort continued into the twentieth century, but went into a progressive decline after the First World War. This unusual photograph was taken in about 1914 in the New Private Baths on Stall Street and shows a woman patient undergoing treatment in the four-cell, or Schnee Bath. It used electrical current in combination with mineral water to treat neuritis. (*Bath Museums Service*)

Left: In a further variation on the theme of spa treatment, jets of hot mineral water are sprayed on to a patient in the needle douche at the New Royal Baths (*c*. 1925) in a sort of hydro-massage and heat therapy. (*Bath Museums Service*)

A crowd of onlookers watch intently as a pair of steamrollers weight-test Cleveland Bridge in April 1928, after a comprehensive programme of strengthening work had been completed. Beyond on the high pavement is Walcot Parade, and on the right, beyond the toll-house, is the Eastern Dispensary. (*Raymond Tate*)

Taken from a house in Walcot Parade, this remarkable photograph shows the large crowd that assembled to witness the freeing of Cleveland Bridge from tolls by the Marquess of Bath on 22 June 1919. (*Bath Reference Library*)

Traffic congestion in Cheap Street (looking east) during the 1930s shows that the phenomenon is not peculiar to the late twentieth century. Behind the traffic lights on the right are Hepworth's the outfitters, and next door, Titley Son & Price, the gentlemen's tailors. Beyond the Pump Room Passage is Shore & Son's shoe shop. The tram in the picture (destined for the Glasshouse on Combe Down) is passing David Greig the provision merchants. At the far end on the corner of Wade's Passage is W.J. Cornish the butcher. (*Bath Reference Library*)

A rainy morning in Union Street during the 1930s – all we know is that the photograph was taken on 'Wednesday. Time 11.25 a.m.' On the left are Barratt's (boot and shoe manufacturers, recently closed down), Samuel's (jewellers), and J. Lyons' café. On the right-hand side of the street is Colmer's department store, Lipton's (grocers), Fox-Andrews (grocers) and beyond, in Stall Street, the Grand Pump Room Hotel, the mineral water fountain, and McIlroy's shop. (*Bath Reference Library*)

Westgate Street in the 1930s. On the left can be seen the Grand Pump Room Hotel Wine Vaults, Archard's the tobacconist, with Oliver's shoe shop beyond. Next is the Oak Café, and next door but one, Arthur's (formerly Rivlin's) Stores on the corner of St Michael's Passage, adjacent to the Grapes Hotel. On the right of the picture is the Angel Hotel (now renamed the Westgate Inn) where James Joyce (Lord Haw-Haw) once stayed before the Second World War. (*Bath Reference Library*)

The Upper Rooms, later known as the Assembly Rooms, are pictured here in about 1931, at which time they were used as a cinema. The placards advertise Bebe Daniels and Ricardo Cortez in *The Maltese Falcon* (the first of three versions to be made), and Margot Grahame in *The Rosary*. (*Bath Reference Library*)

Flags and bunting adorn Milsom Street as Bath celebrates the Silver Jubilee of King George V in 1935. A series of spectacles were arranged to mark the occasion, including gymnastics displays on the Rec and processions in the Royal Victoria Park. (*Bath City Archives*)

Passengers board the electric tram for Combe Down in High Street on a fine morning in 1925. The lady is wearing a long dress reminiscent of the Victorian era, a fashion continued by many elderly ladies until well into the 1930s. The tram carries an advertisement for the Wiltshire bacon of Harris's of Calne. (*Bath Reference Library*)

Bath Abbey bell-ringers prepare to ring in celebration of the coronation of King George VI and Queen Elizabeth, 12 May 1937. Back row, left to right: S. Woodburn, F. Merrett, W.J. Prescott (Tower Master), M. Smart. Front row: Miss N.G. Williams, Mrs A. Evans, T.F. King, H.D. Taylor, H.W. Brown, G. Hawkins, J. Hallett, T. Grant. (*Bath Abbey/Eric Naylor*)

Poised for the downbeat, the Pump Room Orchestra is pictured here in the Concert Room in the late 1930s. It was disbanded in 1938 to save money. (*Bath Reference Library*)

An early victim of Bath's planners was the Bath Royal Literary and Scientific Institution, demolished in 1932 to make way for a new road connecting Orange Grove with Pierrepont Street. In the eighteenth century the site was occupied by Thomas Harrison's Long Room (an assembly room) begun in 1708. The portico seen here was added in 1806. In December 1820, the Kingston Rooms (as they were then known) were partially destroyed by fire, but rebuilt four years later as the Royal Literary and Scientific Institution incorporating a portion of the earlier assembly rooms that survived the fire. Below the Institution were Institution Gardens (Harrison's Walks in the eighteenth century), now known as Parade Gardens. (*Bath Reference Library*)

Demolition contractors clear rubble from the Royal Literary and Scientific Institution, 1932. On the site of the Institution, underground public conveniences were constructed, resulting in the vulgar nickname of 'Bog Island' (Parade Gardens) by which the site is known today. (*Raymond Tate*)

A stream of buses at the newly opened Parade Gardens in the mid-1930s. To the left is the balustrade above the underground public conveniences. Behind is Terrace Walk with a greengrocer's shop, a newsagents (still there) and at the end of the terrace, Loraine the milliner. To the left of the Empire Hotel is the old Police Station in Orange Grove that finally closed in 1966 when 'business' was transferred to the new station in Manvers Street. (*Colin Maggs*)

A busy scene along the Grand Parade on Saturday 2 September 1933 as shoppers and day-trippers wait to board buses. Pulteney Bridge is on the right beyond the parapet. The entrance to the market in Newmarket Row is on the left, and above, the dome of the Victoria Art Gallery. In the distance are the piano showrooms of Duck Son & Pinker Ltd. (*Bath Reference Library*)

Buildings in course of demolition at Cat Lane and Dog Lane in the area between Kingsmead Terrace and Green Park in 1930. In the distance (left) can be seen part of Stothert and Pitt's works. The area in the foreground is now occupied by the Kingsmead flats. (*Bath Reference Library*)

On the site of Cat and Dog lanes, Kingsmead East flats are pictured here under construction in 1931. (*Bath City Archives*)

A view of Kingsmead East flats shortly after they were opened during the summer of 1932. (*Bath Reference Library*)

An aerial view of the City of Bath Boys' School during construction at Alexandra Park, 1931. With the introduction of comprehensive education in Bath in the early 1970s, the school became known as Beechen Cliff School. A young evacuee to Bath, who attended the school during the Second World War, achieved lasting fame in 1954 when he ran the first four-minute mile. His name – Roger Bannister (see p. 106). (*Bath Reference Library*)

One of Bath Corporation's pre-war social housing schemes was at Whiteway on the southern heights of the city. This newly completed house at The Oval is typical of the style of dwelling to be found on this development. (*Bath City Archives*)

Stanley Marks
& Werry Ltd
BAKERS.CONFECTIONERS.CATERERS
BATH. TETBURY.
TROWBRIDGE.MALMESBURY.
HOME
OF
CAKES
GL 3869
GL 5093

Dorchester Street from the bottom of Southgate Street. The vans of the bakers Stanley Marks & Werry Ltd, whose shop was in Cheap Street, were a familiar sight around the city in the 1930s and later. On the left-hand side of the street is Hooper & Dark's furnishing showroom and beyond, The South Pole public house; next, George Williams, the monumental mason. On the right are the premises of the City of Bath Electricity Department. During the Second World War an air raid siren was located on the roof of this building. (*Bath Reference Library*)

The Great Western Railway's 'Badminton' class 4–4–0 No 4109 *Monarch* stands at Bath station on 21 May 1929 with a down stopping service. In the background can be seen houses in Claverton Street and St Mark's Church. *Monarch's* days on the GWR were already numbered at this time, for the locomotive was finally withdrawn from service in 1931. (*Colin Maggs*)

The year is 1935, and a policeman directs traffic on the south side of the Old Bridge. Beneath the railway arch is Smith & Elliott, tobacconists. An electric tram, on its way towards Combe Down, is about to pass The Royal Sailor public house on the corner of Wellsway and Holloway. The hoarding on the side of the railway viaduct advertises a production of *The Girl Friend* at the Theatre Royal. (*Bath Reference Library*)

En route to Newbridge Hill, Motorman Len Hancock on tram car 34 pauses at the Old Bridge on 11 April 1939 to use the 'point bar'. Beyond and to the right are the Electricity Works. (*Colin Maggs*)

The Second World War

Mr G.W. Barrow, Charge Officer at St John's (Bathwick) Depot Casualty Service, and Mr R.C. Chapman, a Party Leader, October 1941. (*Bath Chronicle*)

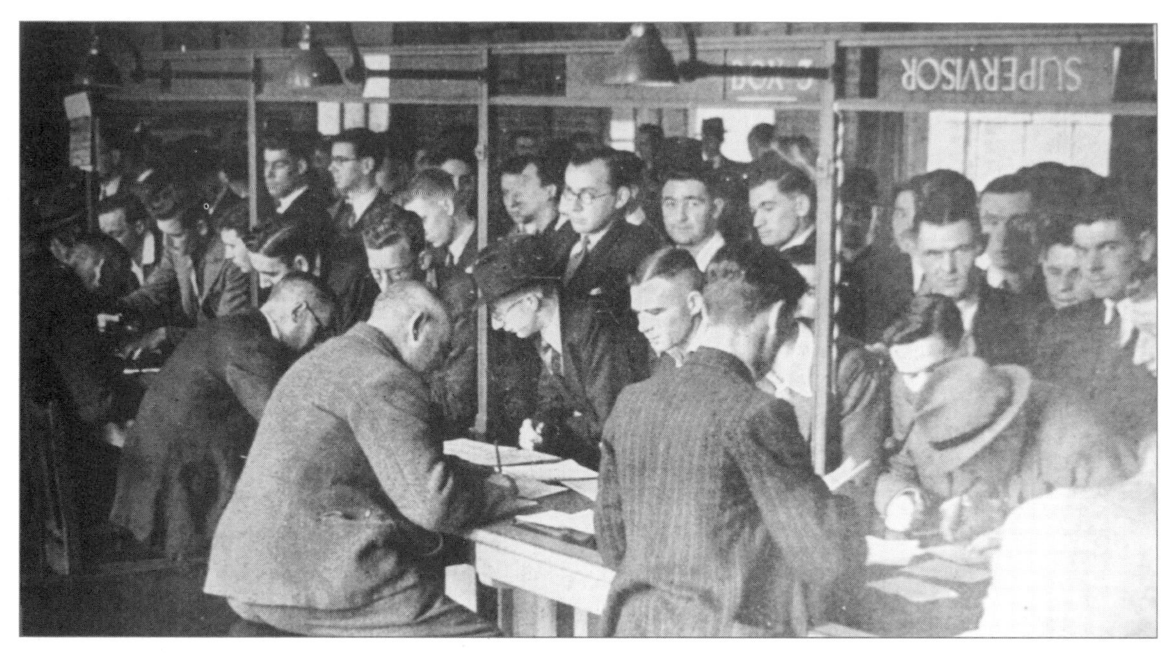

'Bath shall not burn.' Volunteers line up to register for fire-watching duties at Bath Employment Exchange in James Street West early in the war. The Exchange suffered during the blitz and to this day its walls bear the scars of bomb blast and shrapnel damage. (*Bath Chronicle*)

Bath was one of the designated reception areas for wartime evacuees from major British cities thought to be at risk from bombing. At the outbreak of war the city received 7,000 children from London; some of the younger ones were accompanied by their mothers. Here, an evacuee baby is fitted with clothing by members of the WVS. Bags of clothing donated by Bath residents can be seen in the background. (*Bath Reference Library*)

Another shift over, workers stream out of Stothert & Pitt's Victoria works during the war. This Bath engineering firm was heavily committed to supporting the nation's war effort. It manufactured tank turrets and gun mountings for the Army, specialist equipment for the Royal Navy (see p. 68), and hundreds of concrete mixers for use in airfield construction for the RAF. (*Bath City Archives*)

Ready for action: Bath LMS Home Guard Platoon at the Midland station, Green Park, 1941. (*Colin Maggs*)

Bath Rugby team: a wartime XV at their opening match of the season on the Rec in 1942. With the presence of military units in the neighbourhood, there was no knowing who might turn up to play for the local team. Three international caps were in the Bath side in 1942. (*Bath Chronicle*)

One of 'The Few': Pilot Officer Hilary Edridge flew Spitfires with 222 Squadron in the Battle of Britain. The son of a Bath doctor in Gay Street, he died from wounds received in action in October 1940. (*Ione Denny*)

An early wartime street scene near Seven Dials car park in which an air raid shelter had been built. The Theatre Royal and Garrick's Head public house can be seen in the background. (*Bath Reference Library*)

Wartime advertisements on hoardings at Ladywell in Walcot Street. Among the commercial advertisements for cigarettes and Oxo cubes are official Ministry of Information ads warning of the dangers from incendiary bombs, encouragement to join in the war savings campaign, and urging people to conserve fuel to help the war effort. (*Bath City Archives*)

On parade: officers and men of 5th Somerset (Bath City) Battalion, Home Guard, parade on the Rec early in the war. Bath had two battalions of Home Guard: the 5th (Bath City) and the 6th (Bath Admiralty), numbering some 2,700 men in total at their stand-down in 1944. (*Authors*)

One of Bath's two Ford emergency food vans pictured crossing Cleveland Bridge, September 1943. They were part of a fleet of 350 vehicles presented to Britain by Henry Ford to help with emergency feeding following air raids. The two Bath vans were manned by WVS drivers and attendants. (*Kingsmead Motor Co.*)

Stothert & Pitt, the Bath engineering firm, designed and manufactured the two-man human torpedo ('Chariot') for the Royal Navy. The Royal Navy Chariot was a 22-ft long torpedo-shaped submersible with a detachable explosive warhead attached to its nose. It was propelled by a small motor and 'driven' by a pair of frogmen who rode astride its back. (*Authors*)

Bath suffered two nights of bombing over the weekend of 25–27 April 1942. The so-called 'Baedeker' blitz (see introduction p. 15) claimed the lives of over 400 people and injured many hundreds more. St Andrew's Church is seen here from Rivers Street, well ablaze on the second night of the Baedeker blitz, 27 April. The gutted shell was later demolished. (*Bath Chronicle*)

Devastation caused by a high explosive bomb in the Upper Bristol Road near the bottom of Marlborough Lane during the blitz. The hoarding on the wall of the wrecked building exhorts Bathonians to 'Dig for Victory Now'. (*Bath Chronicle*)

Children play on a bombsite at the west end of Julian Road. Catharine Place can be seen in the distance in the gap between the houses. (*Bath Reference Library*)

Mrs Elizabeth Dick, aged 101, who was bombed out of Belvedere, tells the Mayor, Councillor Aubrey Bateman: 'Between ourselves, Hitler thought he'd frightened me – but he didn't.' (*Bath Chronicle*)

Spectators at Bear Flat survey the bomb damage following the devastating raids of 25–27 April 1942. The shops on this corner of Wellsway and Wells Road were later demolished. (*Bath Reference Library*)

The house adjacent to St Mary's Roman Catholic church at the bottom of Burlington Street received a direct hit during the blitz. Air Raid Warden Alexander MacDougall (seventy-eight) of 13 Rivers Street was killed while sheltering in the doorway of the house. All of his personal possessions were looted. (*Bath Chronicle*)

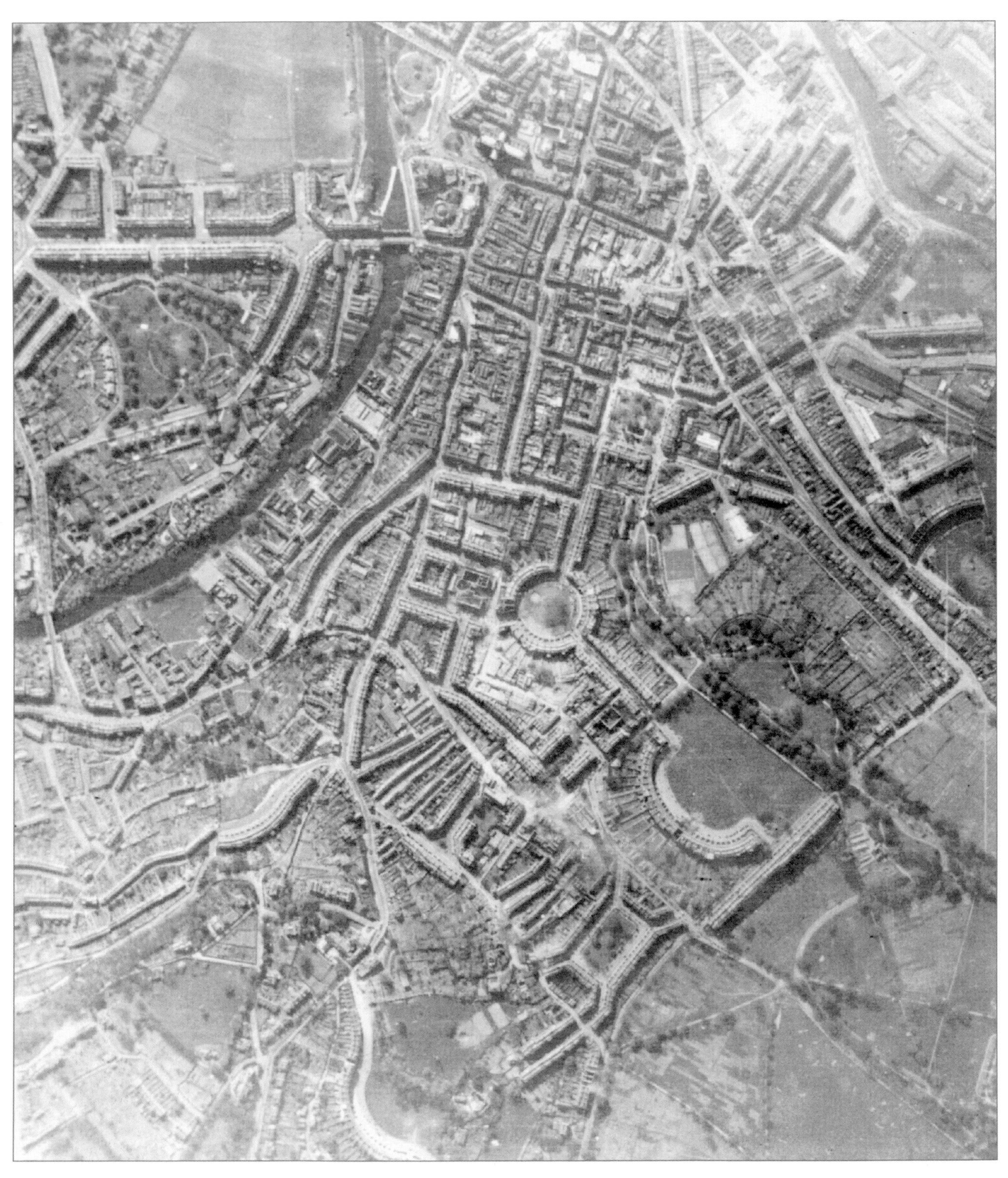

A rare view of the bomb-damaged city taken by an RAF reconnaissance aircraft on the morning of 27 April 1942. At the top of the picture is the Recreation Ground, with the Abbey to the right, and Pulteney Street and Laura Place. At the centre is the Circus (with bomb crater) and the Royal Crescent to the right. At the bottom of the picture is Lansdown Crescent. (*RAF photo/Bath Reference Library*)

Convalescent soldiers at St Martin's Hospital on Combe Down pose for the camera on VJ-Day in 1945. (*Bob White*)

Home from the war: soldiers and sailors are among the happy guests at a children's street party in Hanover Street to celebrate victory in Europe. Street parties were a common feature of the victory celebrations in 1945. Bath lost nearly 600 servicemen and Civil Defence personnel during the Second World War. (*Bath Chronicle*)

These children were among those on the first postwar exchange between Bath and Alkmaar, its twin city in the Netherlands. The boy in the centre is Gordon Banks. (*Gordon Banks*)

Peace restored: a postwar scene in Union Street looking towards Stall Street. The Mineral Water Hospital (right) displays an appeal board – it had suffered serious bomb damage in the blitz. (*Bath Chronicle*)

You've Never Had It So Good

A postwar view up Union Street towards James Colmer's department store. (*Bath Reference Library*)

Sir Patrick Abercrombie's *Plan for Bath* was unveiled to the public at the beginning of February 1945 in an exhibition of models, maps, drawings and photographs. His far-sighted plan was concerned not only with the building of new houses and conversion of older ones in the city, but the routing of traffic and proposals for public and industrial buildings. (*Authors*)

Bath City Council in session at the Guildhall on 29 October 1946. The Mayor (Councillor Clements) is flanked by Councillor Plowman and the Town Clerk (J.Basil Ogden). (*Bath Reference Library*)

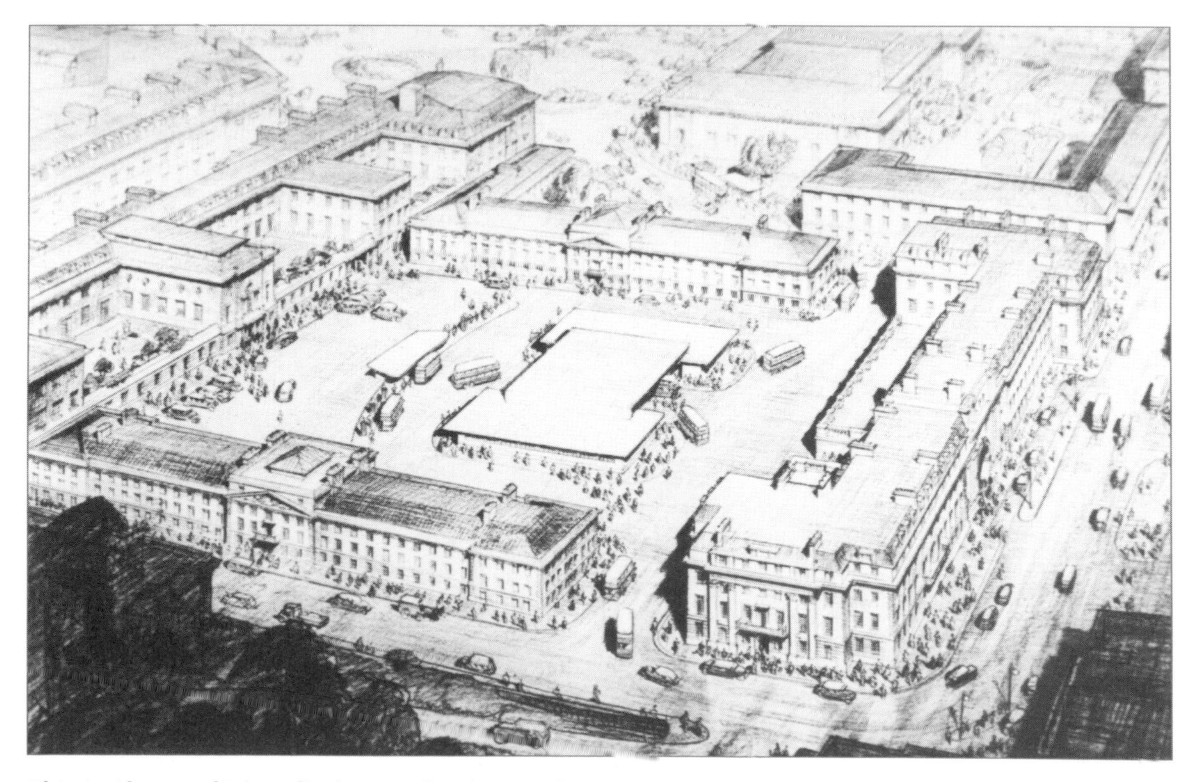

This is Abercrombie's radical vision for the new bus station, pictured from the roof of Bath Spa railway station. Compare this attractive solution with the ugly concrete bus station the city finally received. (*Bath City Archives*)

His plan also included exciting new ideas for Northgate and a proposed riverside development along Walcot Street. (*Bath City Archives*)

Traffic congestion in George Street, October 1945. Although the war was over, petrol rationing remained in force until well into the 1950s. (*Bath City Archives*)

This 1952 view of Seven Dials and Westgate Street, remains largely unaltered in the late 1990s. The County Wine Vaults is now an Irish 'theme' pub. (*Bath Reference Library*)

Flooding in Southgate Street in March 1947. At the centre of the picture is the Odeon (formerly the Regal) cinema, with the Oliver bar next door. Above the cinema is The Blackett Press. (*Colin Maggs/Bath Reference Library*)

The Broad Quay under flood, March 1947. At left, swans are being fed from Ben Butcher's refreshment stall close to the Old Bridge. On the other side of the river can be seen bus shelters on the Lower Bristol Road. (*Colin Maggs/Bath Reference Library*)

STEAD & SIMPSON LTD
DR. SCHOLLS
FOOT COMFORT
SERVICE
FOX ANDREWS LTD
LIPTON
GL 1913
GL 3246

An early postwar view of Union Street Just visible (left) is Fox-Andrews, the grocers (on the corner of Union Street and Westgate Street). Above, Lipton's, the grocers, and further up, James Colmer's department store. At the top of the picture is The Don where many Bath children were taken to be kitted out with their school uniforms. Top right of the street is Barratt's shoe shop, then Peacock the fishmongers (whose sign is visible). In 1954, Colmer's sold the freehold of their premises to the National Coal Board Pension Fund for £310,000. The sale was one of the biggest property deals negotiated in Bath up to this time. Colmer's leased the premises back from the NCB. (*Bath Reference Library*)

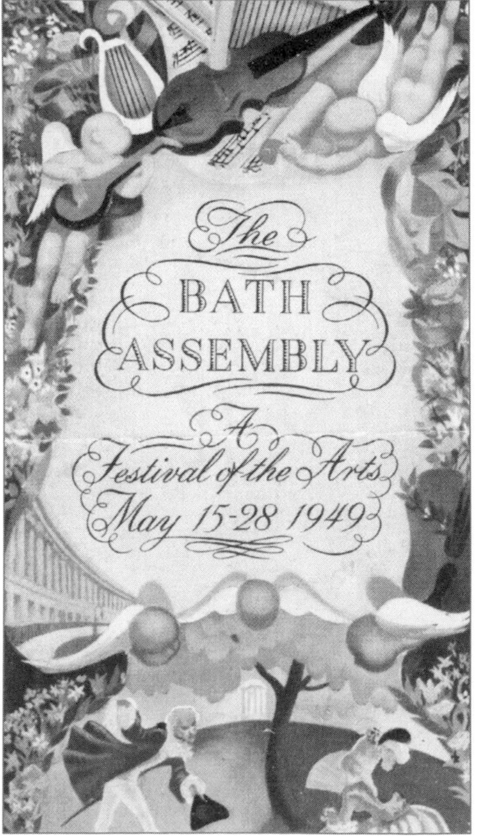

Above: Haile Selassie, Emperor of Ethiopia (1892–1975), was exiled to Bath in the late 1930s after the Italians conquered his country. He and his family lived at Fairfield, Newbridge Hill, but he returned to Ethiopia in May 1941 once the Italian invaders had been expelled. In October 1954, the emperor revisited England for a state visit during which he travelled to Bath where the Freedom of the City was conferred on him. In this photograph, taken on 18 October, Haile Selassie discusses the architectural splendour of the Abbey with the Rector, Archdeacon Edwin Cook. Also in the picture, left to right, the Abbey's Head Verger (Bert Marquess), members of the emperor's entourage, the Mayor of Bath (Councillor William Gallop) and the Mayoress. (*Bath Chronicle*)

Left: A Bath festival was proposed for 1939, but abandoned because of the threat of war. It was not until three years after the war that a festival of the arts was held in the city under the artistic direction of Ian Hunter; it was called 'The Bath Assembly' (borrowing an eighteenth-century expression), and was held between 21 April and 1 May 1948. A further Assembly was held in the following year, this time with the honorary artistic director, John Boddington. Organised by Bath Assembly Ltd, in conjunction with the Arts Council of Great Britain, it was under the patronage of Princess Margaret, the present queen's sister. In 1955, Sir Thomas Beecham was one of three artistic directors of 'The Bath May Festival'. With the exception of 1956 and 1957, a Bath Festival, as it was later known, has been held every year since 1948. (*Authors*)

Postwar housing development at Twerton saw the western suburbs of Bath pushed further outwards. Here, new homes are under construction at Freeview Road, Twerton, in 1950. (*Bath Reference Library*)

Clearing Snow Hill in preparation for building the controversial new flats, September 1954. Work is about to begin on driving test piles into the ground. (*Bath City Archives*)

A Sparrow's crane puts the finishing touches to a new traffic roundabout at the junction of Southgate Street and St James's Parade in the late 1950s. Sparrow's cranes were a familiar sight in Bath for many years and the Sparrow story, which began in the 1920s, took off after the end of the Second World War when building in Britain got into full swing again. By the 1970s the family-run business had developed into one of Britain's largest mobile crane hire specialists, with more than 1,000 employees worldwide. Today the company is part of the Rentokil Initial group, but the Sparrow family maintains an active involvement in its subsidiary GWS Crane Hire, of which Sparrow's is a constituent part. (*Gordon Sparrow*)

The Changing Face of Bath

A scene of dereliction at the bottom of Chatham Row in the late 1970s. (*Authors*)

A great programme of restoration work on the fabric of the Abbey was carried out between 1947 and 1960. Following its completion, Queen Elizabeth, the Queen Mother, visited the Abbey on 22 March 1960 for a special service of thanksgiving. (*Bath Chronicle*)

In December 1960, the worst floods since 1882 caused chaos in many parts of the city bordering the Avon. Heavy rainfall during the first four days of December caused the river to rise 20 ft above its normal level at Pulteney weir, and for the first time since 1947 Southgate Street was flooded. St John's Road and Henrietta Street were also flooded to a depth of 6 ft. The floods resulted in considerable material loss to industrial and trading premises as well as homes, chiefly on the city side of the river. In this view looking downstream from the Old Bridge the premises of Bladwell's and Tucker's Hay & Corn Stores have suffered the effects of the flooding. (*Bath Chronicle*)

An Army lorry helps ferry pedestrians through deep floodwater at the bottom of Southgate Street. (*Bath Chronicle*)

Once the floods had subsided, the great cleaning-up operation gathered pace and saw young and old turning to with mops and pails. (*Bath Chronicle*)

A cold snap that began on the night of Boxing Day 1962 continued without let-up across much of the country until the following February. Blizzard conditions followed by a big freeze caused serious disruption to daily life in Bath. The river froze over at Bathwick, and 24 January went down in the record books as the coldest day ever recorded in Bath (for any month or year) at minus 5° Celsius. Thanks to the big freeze, Bath's Theatre Royal had the greatest number of cancellations in living memory, and the pantomime *Mother Goose* was cut short. In this gloomy photograph, taken from Brunswick Place in January 1963, Christ Church can be seen nestling beneath a mantle of snow and ice. (*Authors*)

Sadly, this fine early eighteenth-century town house at 24 High Street became a victim of Bath City Council's relentless drive to demolish and 'redevelop' areas of the city. It is seen here in July 1963 when occupied by George Oliver's boot and shoe shop, but fell to the developer's ball and chain the following year. The adjoining properties between this house and the corner of Upper Borough Walls, occupied by Cater, Stoffell & Fortt ('The Stores') were also demolished. (*Brian Newman*)

The group of buildings seen above that replaced Oliver's and adjoining properties can only be described as uninspired and incongruous. Oliver's and Manfield's moved elsewhere in the city, but Cater's remained on the site until 1984. For many its closure marked the end of an era in Bath's retail history. Today, the site is occupied by the C & A chain-store and smaller shops. (*Authors*)

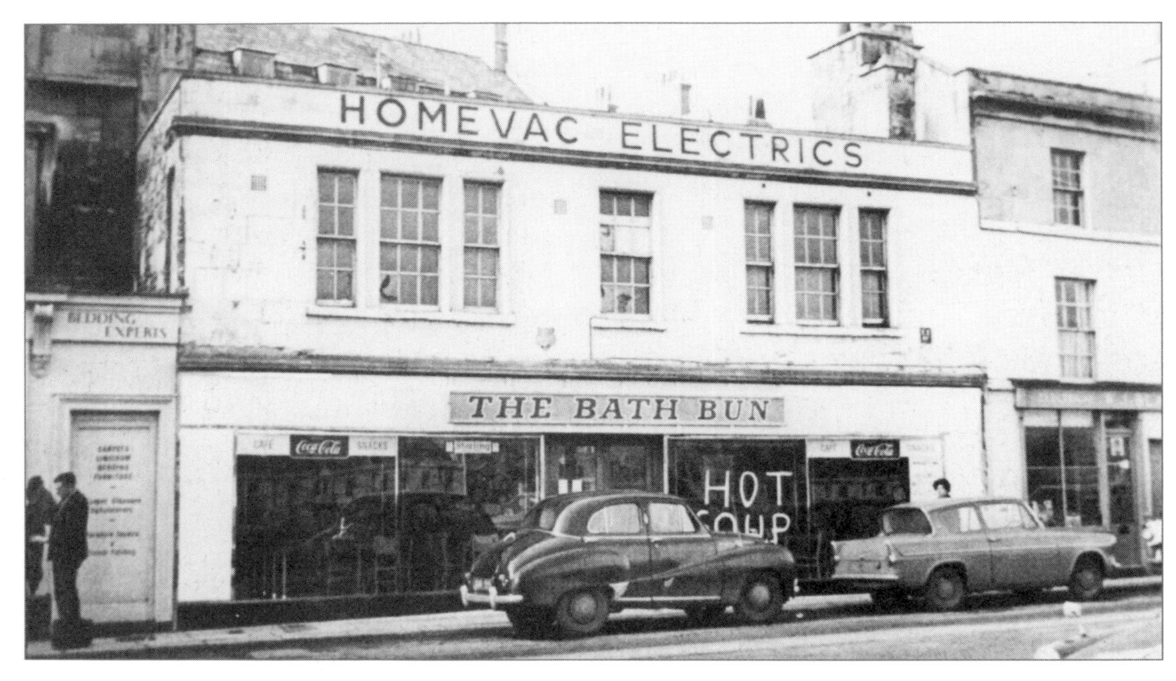

Walcot Street, 1961. Homevac Electrics and the Bath Bun café have long since gone and the premises are now occupied by Knickerbean and a charity shop. On the right of the picture can be seen the shop of W.J. Blackmore, electrical contractor, now occupied by the Bath Hatter. (*Bath City Archives*)

Left: Fortt's café, Green Street, 1961. Today, the splendid glass frontage has been altered and this corner of Green Street is now home to The Oliver public house and restaurant. Next door in Broad Street is George Gregory's second hand bookshop. (*Bath City Archives*)

Below right: This rare view of the Pump Room was taken from Westgate Street following the demolition of the Grand Pump Room Hotel in neighbouring Stall Street, January 1960. During the war years, the hotel was requisitioned by the Admiralty and used for a time by the Battleship Section of the Director of Naval Construction. After the war it enjoyed a brief but unexceptional revival as a hotel in the late 1950s before it was demolished during 1958–9 to make way for the Arlington House development of shops and flats. (*Authors*)

Far right: The Grapes Hotel in Westgate Street, pictured here on 12 May 1962, remains intact to this day and continues to trade as a public house. Next door can be seen the tobacconist and confectionery shop of Miss Mary Sidwell, and further along the street is the shop of Frank Phillips, the hairdresser, and Tiani's café and milkbar – all now long since gone. (*Authors*)

Broad Street, 1961. At centre left is Monk & Co., baby carriage dealers and toy shop, Ware's garage (distributors for Standard and Triumph cars), Alan Coward, watchmaker, and James Payne, bootmaker. (*Bath City Archives*)

SEVERN – WESSEX
EXPRESS
53807

During the 1960s Dr Beeching, who was employed by the government to rationalise the British railway system, swung his axe, and at a stroke Bath lost one of its two principal railway stations with the closure of Green Park (the 'Midland'). Pictured here in happier days, a former Somerset & Dorset 7F steam locomotive passes Bath Junction after leaving Green Park, hauling a 'down' Ian Allan-sponsored Severn–Wessex express excursion. (*Colin Maggs*)

Oldfield Girls' School, in a new rural setting at Kelston Road, was opened in 1957. It replaced the old school building in Wellsway. (*Bath Reference Library*)

The origins of the University of Bath can be traced to the Bristol Trade School of 1856 and its offspring, Bristol College of Technology (1949–60). In the latter year, the college was divided into Bristol College of Science and Technology and Bristol Technical College. Six years later, Bristol College of Science and Technology was transformed into the University of Bath. There was some public disquiet in 1964 when it was revealed that Bath City Council had offered the 141-acre Norwood Playing Fields site (purchased by public subscription) on a 999-year lease at a peppercorn rent (excluding rates) to enable the university to be built. At the time the city council gave an assurance that alternative playing fields in Bath would be provided. (*Bath University via Michael Painting*)

Yehudi Menuhin (1916–99), who was associated with the Bath Festival from 1959 to 1968, is seen here receiving the Freedom of the City of Bath in 1965 from the Mayor, Councillor Mrs Elsie Hanna. (*Bath Chronicle*)

The composer Michael Tippett (1905–98), who was artistic director of the Bath Festival from 1969 to 1974, lived in Wiltshire. (*Bath Chronicle*)

The legendary American rock guitarist Jimi Hendrix (1942–70) who performed at The Pavilion in 1968, is seen here backstage. (*Bath Chronicle*)

At the end of the Second World War, Bath's nearby RAF station at Colerne became a maintenance base, but regained something of its former prestige in 1952 when Fighter Command returned and the station was used to train night-fighter aircrews. Five years later, Colerne was taken over by Transport Command, and the first Handley Page Hastings transport aircraft arrived. For the next ten years, Colerne's three squadrons of Hastings became a familiar sight in the skies over Bath as they flew off to the four corners of the earth along the famous Transport Command routes. Here is a Hastings of No. 36 Squadron at Colerne in 1968.

In addition to the flying display programme, Colerne's fine collection of historic aircraft were wheeled out on-to the flight line for static display alongside the RAF's latest aircraft types. Here, a Second World War German Messerschmitt Me 163 Komet rocket-powered fighter plane shares the crowds at Colerne's 1972 display with a Lockheed C-130 Hercules aircraft of RAF Lyneham's Transport Wing. RAF Colerne was closed in 1976 as a result of defence cuts. However, as Azimghur Barracks it is currently occupied by the Army's 21 Signals Regiment.

This gloomy picture of demolition in Southgate Street was taken from the Electricity Board building in Dorchester Street in October 1971. The site was being cleared to make way for a redevelopment scheme that eventually gave Bath its ugly and soul-less Southgate shopping precinct. Today, Boots the Chemist occupies much of the site in the foreground. (*Bath Chronicle*)

A busy Southgate Street showing the Co-op's 'Television Corner' at the junction with Dorchester Street, 1961. Further up Southgate Street can be seen the premises of Bath Pram & Toy Shop. (*Bath City Archives*)

A Sparrow's mobile crane lifts an inspection basket into the Roman Baths from Stall Street. The fountain in the foreground has since been moved to Parade Gardens. (*Gordon Sparrow*)

In the early 1960s it was decided to construct a new outer ring road from Green Park to the Old Bridge along the Broad Quay. The plan coincided with the implementation of a flood protection scheme announced in 1962. The Old Bridge, which occupied the site of a river crossing in use from Roman (or even earlier) times, was demolished, and replaced by the Churchill Bridge a little way downstream. Piecemeal development on the old Broad Quay site continued into the 1970s. A prosaic design for an office block known as Carpenter House (seen here in December 1972) replaced a building formerly occupied by Bladwell's. It was used by the Admiralty as office accommodation. (*Bath Chronicle*)

Redevelopment of the Seven Dials site in the early 1970s failed to provide the aesthetically pleasing design solution that this busy corner of Bath cried out for. The Mecca dancehall and nightclub (opened during the latter part of 1974) occupied this prime position for some years and the flat roof was later transformed into a garden centre. (*Bath Chronicle*)

This unusual view, photographed from the Empire Hotel in 1967, shows Orange Grove, Terrace Walk and the Parade Gardens bus terminus. The triangular area to the left of the picture was originally occupied by the early nineteenth-century Royal Literary and Scientific Institution. It was demolished in 1932–3 to make way for a new road linking Orange Grove with Pierrepont Street and public conveniences. Today, this one-time site of erudition serves as a bus terminus; the toilets have long since been closed. They were later converted into the Island Club – a nightclub which is also now defunct. (Bath Reference Library)

On 9 August 1973, thirteen years after the visit of Queen Elizabeth the Queen Mother, her daughter Queen Elizabeth II, accompanied by the Duke of Edinburgh, attended a thanksgiving service in Bath Abbey to commemorate 1,000 years of monarchy. Edgar, the first king of all England, was crowned in the Saxon Abbey (which stood on the site of the present church) on Whitsun Day 973, by Dunstan, Archbishop of Canterbury, assisted by Oswald, Archbishop of York. (*Bath Chronicle*)

Modern Bath

Central Bath in September 1998 showing the Abbey, Guildhall, Victoria Art Gallery, Market, Pulteney Bridge, the Empire and Orange Grove. (*Janet Rayner*)

Bath's fastest knight, Roger Bannister (b.1929), returned to the city in 1984 to receive an honorary doctorate from the Universiy of Bath. On 6 May 1954, Bannister, an old boy of the City of Bath Boy's School (now Beechen Cliff School), became the first man in the world to run a mile in under four minutes. (*Bath Chronicle*)

Fireworks illuminate the night sky over the Royal Crescent in a spectacular display during Bath's Walt Disney Festival, September 1983. (*Bath Chronicle*)

The Royal Crescent is also the backdrop to this colourful re-enactment of the Battle of Lansdown by the Sealed Knot on 16 September 1984. (*Authors*)

Warmly wrapped against the winter chill, a local brass band plays carols and other seasonal music to entertain passers-by in Stall Street during a Saturday pre-Christmas shopping spree in 1980. (*Authors*)

For many years street entertainment has been a feature of the Bath scene. Here, Jim Couza, from the United States, plays his hammered dulcimer in Union Street to entertain shoppers in May 1984. (*Bath Chronicle*)

This maze in Sydney Gardens was made in 1805, the year of Nelson's victory over the French and Spanish fleets at Trafalgar, and removed in 1840, shortly after Queen Victoria came to the throne. (*Authors*)

Continuing the tradition, the Beazer maze at Spring Gardens was constructed in 1984 to echo the theme of the Bath Festival that year. It is seen here from the roof of a house in Johnstone Street. (*Authors*)

The changing face of central Bath. When the Royal Baths were demolished and the old spa treatment centre gutted, both were completely rebuilt in 1988 in the guise of yet another shopping arcade, named the Colonnades. For a number of reasons the arcade did not attract the level of custom needed for its many and varied shops to survive, and within a few years, with only a few firms still trading, it closed. The Tourist Information Office had been relocated to the Colonnades from its long standing home in Abbey Church Yard, but it too faced a significant drop in use due to its new location. Thankfully, common sense prevailed and it has now returned to more suitable premises in Abbey Church Yard. British Home Stores now occupies the Colonnades. (*Both photographs: Authors*)

After the demolition in the 1970s of shops and offices in Northgate (including John R.Huntley, the Tramways Office, and Foyle's Furnishings), the site opposite the General Post Office and adjacent to the Hilton (formerly Beaufort) Hotel in Walcot Street remained an eyesore until its redevelopment in the late 1980s. (*Authors*)

The result of the Northgate-Walcot Street development was the Podium shopping centre which represents a fair attempt at combining late twentieth-century style with that of Bath's classical heritage. (Compare it with the Abercrombie plan for the Northgate area on pp. 80–1.) It also shows how far the attitudes of Bath's planners have come since the 1960s, with the design travesty of the Podium's close neighbour, the Hilton Hotel, plain to see. In addition to the Waitrose supermarket and a number of other traders on the ground floor, the first floor has several restaurants; it also houses the Central and Reference Libraries under one roof. The spacious underground car park on a number of levels has proved inadequate for the ever-increasing numbers of shoppers' cars. (*Authors*)

The 'Great Storm' that swept across Britain on the morning of 25 January 1990 left a trail of death and destruction in its wake. Compared with other areas of the country, Bath got off relatively lightly. Nevertheless, the city and its inhabitants suffered their share of trouble. Gale force winds devastated buildings, uprooted trees, tore down power lines, and toppled lorries as though they were children's toys. People suffered serious injury from falling masonry, and cars were crushed beneath the trunks of fallen trees. The Royal Victoria Park and the Botanical Gardens suffered the loss of some of their oldest tree and plant specimens. (*Bath Chronicle*)

The British dislike of unfair taxation is a tradition that stretches back to the fourteenth century. Across the country, hatred of the Tory government's Poll Tax (euphemistically called the Community Charge) boiled over into civil disobedience in March 1990, and in London and elsewhere demonstrators were involved in violent clashes with the police. The tax meant that the old system of rates (i.e. a single tax based on the rateable value of a property) was scrapped in favour of a personal tax on each member of a household. Many people (the elderly among them) who refused to pay the Poll Tax, were sentenced to terms of imprisonment – an act that further inflamed the highly volatile climate of public opinion. Here on 13 March 1990, Labour members of Bath City Council vote with their feet and leave the Council Chamber as the Poll Tax is being set. (*Bath Chronicle*)

Outside the Guildhall in High Street, demonstrators holding placards and banners make their protest against the unfairness of the Poll Tax. The tax was abolished in 1991 and replaced by a council tax based on property values and size of households. (*Bath Chronicle*)

The tension here is almost palpable as Chris Patten (the sitting Tory MP for Bath since 1979 and national chairman of the Conservative Party) and the relatively unknown Don Foster (the Liberal Democrat candidate) sweat it out at the Guildhall as the count is awaited following the General Election on 9 April 1992. Patten lost his seat and Foster was returned with a majority of 3,768 (25,718 votes were polled). (*Bath Liberal Democrats*)

For many years the residents of Batheaston campaigned for a bypass to relieve the heavy traffic congestion that had bedevilled their narrow main street, part of the A4. They were successful. But when work began in March 1994 to solve Batheaston's traffic nightmare, the problem was merely shifted elsewhere. A huge scar was gouged in the landscape to carry the new road from Bathford to Lambridge and to the east of Little Solsbury towards Upper Swainswick where it joins the A46. Thousands of acres of prime farmland were despoiled, and homes that stood in the path of the new road were subjected to compulsory purchase and then demolished. Horrified by the environmental impact of the road, people from Bath and elsewhere demonstrated in an attempt to stop what they believed to be sheer madness. Violent scenes were witnessed as a hard core of demonstrators took on the police and site security guards in an attempt to delay the work. (*Bath Chronicle*)

Despite a public enquiry and the best efforts of the objectors to the scheme – the majority of them passive demonstrators – work went ahead, and the road was completed in July 1996. This blot is plain for all to see: another sign of how man's love affair with the internal combustion engine is responsible for the desecration of beautiful countryside. (*Authors*)

The Abbey nave in 1996, looking east, during the great programme of cleaning and conservation. The maze of scaffolding was itself a work of art. (*Authors*)

As part of the Bath Abbey 2000 campaign, the Friends of Bath Abbey were responsible for the cleaning and conservation of the West Front at a cost of £288,000. (*Bath Abbey*)

Bath's tour buses are a familiar but often unwelcome sight around the city today. Complaints from residents about the air and noise pollution they generate has caused lively correspondence in the *Bath Chronicle*. (*Authors*)

In 1998, tourism generated £184 million for Bath and provided employment for more than 6,000 people in local businesses. The city received more than 1.8 million day trippers and almost one million overnight visitors in the same year. (*Authors*)

The Roman Baths (the King's Bath is pictured here) are the fourth largest tourist attraction in the United Kingdom (the Tower of London is the first). Each year they attract almost a million visitors who come to see one of the best-preserved Roman bathing complexes in the world. (*Authors*)

Bath's renaissance as a spa resort started to take shape on the site of the old Beau Street and Hot Baths in 1999. When completed, the multi-million pound scheme will provide spa facilities on five floors within the new complex including a main spa pool, therapy pools and treatment rooms. (*Authors*)

Bath's original Theatre Royal was in Orchard Street (now the Masonic Hall) where some of the most celebrated actors and actresses of their day performed until the theatre finally closed in 1805. After much discussion at the turn of the century the foundation stone of Bath's new Theatre Royal in Beaufort Square was laid in August 1804. Alas, a fire on Good Friday 1852 gutted the building. The rebuilt theatre opened in March of the following year with a performance of *A Midsummer Night's Dream*. The present entrance in Sawclose (pictured) was a later addition to the building. (*Authors*)

Living with mistakes of the past: insensitive postwar redevelopment effectively blocked off the crossroads where Kingsmead Street, Charles Street and New King Street met. In this 1999 view from New King Street looking towards Charles Street, the incongruity of the 1960s telephone exchange is all too apparent. (*Authors*)

Plans for the future: Kensington bus depot on the London Road was sold in 1999 for redevelopment as a supermarket. The Safeway store that will occupy the site is scheduled for completion in the spring of 2000, but it remains to be seen how the increased traffic it will undoubtedly generate will affect this congested and air-polluted corner of Bath. (*Authors*)

Living to see the future: the Royal United Hospital at Combe Park is undergoing a programme of expansion to provide enhanced health care facilities for Bath and district in the new millennium. (*Annie Falconer*)

Following the tragic death in Paris of Diana, Princess of Wales, in August 1997, there was a spontaneous outpouring of public grief across the country. At Bath, an evening memorial service was held on 5 September in the Abbey which was filled to capacity, and loudspeakers relayed the service to large crowds in Abbey Church Yard and beyond. Over 1,000 people signed the Abbey book of condolence. Following the service a candlelit vigil provided an opportunity for private prayer and meditation, and many people remained in the Abbey for a considerable time. (*Michael Phelp*)

HRH The Prince of Wales was guest of honour at Bath Abbey's service of thanksgiving and commemoration on 29 June 1999, marking the 500th anniversary of the present Abbey and the successful completion of the Bath Abbey 2000 refurbishment campaign. Prince Charles is seen here with Sally Langdon. (*Bath Abbey*)

In 1998, Bath Rugby Football Club travelled to Bordeaux where they played against Brive in the greatest game in the club's history. Some 5,000 supporters made the trip to France to see their team win a penalty which Jon Callard converted to give his side the lead. Then, two minutes into injury time, Brive missed a penalty of their own, handing Bath victory in the European Cup with a score of 19–18. (*Bath Chronicle*)

Acknowledgements and Picture Credits

Most of the photographs reproduced in this book have been obtained from the collections held in the City Archives at the Guildhall, at Bath Reference Library in The Podium, and from the *Bath Chronicle* offices at Windsor Bridge. These photographs are reproduced here by kind permission of their owners. A number of photographs have come from private collections and permission to reproduce these images is also gratefully acknowledged.

In particular the authors would like to thank the following individuals for their help in the preparation of this book and for the loan of photographs: Liz Bevan, Bath Reference Library; Colin Johnston, City Archivist; Katie Lee and Stephany Woodhead, the *Bath Chronicle*; Gordon Sparrow, Sparrow's Crane Hire Ltd; Bath Liberal Democrats; Colin Maggs; Bath Abbey; Annie Falconer; Michael Phelp; John Reynolds; Raymond Tate; Janet Rayner and Michael Painting.

When it comes to photographs of its twentieth century heritage, Bath is at something of a disadvantage when compared to other British cities. In the 1970s the *Bath Chronicle*, for long the source of a wonderful variety of photographs depicting the city at work and play, decided to throw away much of its photo archive. Presumably the rationale was that newspapers were in the business of gathering today's news and not storing yesterday's memories. But whatever the reason, it is plain that a sizeable chunk of Bath's history in photographs has vanished for ever.

Readers will notice that many of the photographs reproduced in this book depict general street scenes in and around the centre of Bath. Many of these were taken by the City Engineer's Department, particularly in the 1930s, to monitor traffic flow and help in the future to devise new road schemes. It would seem, therefore, that Bath has always been afflicted with problems that stem from the motor car. Sadly, we have been unable to include many pictures that show the daily lives of Bathonians, or of the outlying suburbs. This is more a reflection of the range of material available through the principal archive sources in the city than an omission on the part of the authors.

The authors have taken all reasonable steps to trace copyright holders of the photographs reproduced in this book. In a few instances they have been unable to do so. They apologise in advance if anyone's copyright has been accidentally infringed and will be happy to credit them and pay an acceptable reproduction fee in any future edition of this book.